Introduction 3

Chapter One 4

Chapter Two 13

Chapter Three 18

Chapter Four 20

Chapter Five 29

Chapter Six 40

Chapter Seven 43

Chapter Eight 54

Chapter Nine 58

Chapter Ten 60

Introduction

Easy Guide to Self-publishing eBooks is a complete system that will allow you to publish your first eBook and sell it over the Internet.

Be sure you participate in all of the marketing activities mentioned in the Marketing Plan section of the book.

You will achieve success when you follow the directions.

Here is what you need to begin your successful journey in publishing and marketing your eBooks.

1. You need a computer with an Internet connection. For the first few exercises in this book you can borrow time on a computer from a friend or rent computer time at Kinko's or a similar establishment.

2. You need eBook authoring software. All you need right now is Microsoft Word or a program that lets you save ASCII text files. ASCII text files are the same file types as the e-mail messages you send and receive. If you have Adobe Acrobat that would be great, but you don't need it to begin these exercises. Soon you will be able to purchase the Microsoft Reader with Cleartype that may prove to be a great investment for you as well.

3. You need a fax machine, or fax service. You may be able to use a business supply store or print shop like Kinko's. There are also free fax services that allow a minimum amount of faxes for no charge.

4. You need several e-mail accounts. Set up at least 3 separate new free e-mail accounts. You will need one for your business, one for your personal e-mail and one for a return address when you register with search engines and directories. You will get tons of junk mail when you register, so you will need one e-mail account for a dump.

5. You need a desire to adjust to your market place. Try to stay out of a fixed mindset on what a book is supposed to resemble. Allow your paying customers to help it evolve into a masterpiece that they will enjoy. Keep open to formatting and authoring more eBooks in a variety of formats.

Chapter One

Chapter One:

What is an eBook and Why Should I Publish One?

Let me begin with a story...

In December of 1999, as stories of the New Millennium where hitting the newspapers, I was thinking of a way to make my New Year and New Millennium memorable.

What I really wanted to do is find a way to earn money very quickly through writing. I already had an eBook version of my first paper bound book, *How To Hypnotize Yourself Without Losing Your Mind,* which would account for 5 or 10 eBook sales each month. I am only counting sales from my website.

I studied the statistical report of all of my webpages and found that one page consistently had an enormous amount of visitor traffic each month. The page title was *How to Hypnotize Other People.*

How to Hypnotize Other People, was a page that included free information that assists people hypnotizing each other. I found that page had nearly three times as many web visitors than the page hosting my information on self-hypnosis. An alarm went off in my head! Why don't I create and publish an eBook that will teach basic instruction in *How to Hypnotize Other People*?

On December 10, 1999 I did just that and I have never looked back! From December 10 through January 9, or one full month of displaying the eBook on my website, I sold over 100 copies of the new eBook. At a price of $10.00 per eBook I earned $1000.00 in royalties. I kept almost all of it because by selling a book in eBook format, I only had the cost of the credit card processing. This was a small percentage of the total sales.

The first quarter of selling this eBook is now over and sales keep going up and up.

Now I have seven new eBooks and I am going to keep adding more.

You can too! As you read this book you will learn how to sell your eBooks to the world. You will learn how to **publish your brilliance** and have readers respond within an hour. You will learn how to **market your eBooks without spending any money**.

I love the Internet because I find I always have two choices marketing products. I can pay for marketing or I can market for free. Since I advertise my books and eBooks without spending any money, this is the world I am most familiar with. You will first learn how to sell your eBooks from other organizations' websites and then also sell the eBooks from your own. This book includes a detailed marketing plan and winning strategies that will soon have you earning book royalties.

This is a perfect way to start a profitable part time business because all of the contacts you make are by e-mail. You will process orders at convenient times.

You are not making personal sales calls to bookstores or libraries. You do not have to conform to their schedules and their whims.

You can earn money and keep your regular job. I will warn you that you may end up quitting your regular job or profession as you gain expertise in publishing and selling your eBooks.

It is great fun!

What is an eBook?

An eBook or electronic book, or virtual book or digital book is simply a digital text file or group of files that when put together can be read on computers or dedicated eBook reading devices.

eBooks may include text, sound, photographs, illustrations and video. eBooks may contain "hot links" that allow the reader immediate access to web sites referred in the text.

eBooks can be published in a variety of ways:

1. eBooks can be published as digital files that are downloaded and read on laptop or desktop computers. This is the primary type of eBook media discussed in this book.

2. eBooks can be created as digital files that are downloaded and read on palm-top or handheld computers.

3. eBooks can be published as digital files that are downloaded and read on dedicated eBook reader devices such as the Rocketbook eBook Reader or Softbook eBook Reader or the Everybook eBook Reader.

4. eBooks can be digital files that are copied onto floppy disks or a CD-ROMs.

By the time you are read this book, other forms of electronic books may have already appeared. I will keep you up-to-date with eBook updates when you register this book.

Give Me Examples of eBooks

Examples of an eBook would be a 400-page novel, complete with any illustrations or photographs.

An eBook could also be a training manual. A Reiki eBook is one of the best selling eBooks and sells for $20.00 a copy.

An eBook is a 5 page specialized report that focuses on solving a specific problem.

eBooks can be short stories. Instead of buying a collection of short stories by an author you are unfamiliar with, you can now purchase one or two short stories at a time for only a couple of bucks each!

eBooks may be multimedia CD-ROMs with sound, video and text just like all the new encyclopedias that are published today.

Many authors in the main stream are now publishing their books as eBooks. Stephen King and Oprah publish eBooks

Why don't you?

Advantages of Purchasing and Reading eBooks

The eBook serves customers in the following ways:

1. The international customer who does not want to wait a month or longer for the information can now have it shortly after credit card payment is made.

2. The college student who has limited funds for purchasing books can access a computer and can quickly download, print and read information at a very low cost. eBooks generally save the student at least 20% of traditional books.

3. The travelling executive who doesn't want to carry around heavy books in her luggage but wants access to reading a variety of topics can pack a light load.

4. Conservationists love reading this way. eBooks save not only trees in the process, but the associated inks and chemicals as well as oil production in moving those trees to the mills and books into traditional bookstores.

5. Many people want privacy. There are eBooks available that focus on religious, personal hygiene or sexual topics that can be easily downloaded and read without the reader going to a store and bringing an embarrassing title to the attention of the bookstore clerk.

6. Some readers love to use their computers. Even a slower speed, cheaper computer can hold thousands of books on the hard disk. Since there are many titles that can be downloaded for free, many readers can now have a library that competes with their local library.

7. People that have poor eyesight now have the ability of changing the size and shape of all the characters they view on the computer screen. They are not fixed into one font size like a typical paper book.

Once you start publishing your own eBooks you will be more apt to download and purchase them for yourself.

Don't you agree?

What do I write about?

What do you write about? What are your interests in life? What do you do for a living? What lessons in life did you learn that would have value to your fellow man? What are readers interested in reading about?

Take some time and write down answers to these questions. Remember that an eBook can be only 5 pages long or it can be 400 pages long. Whether you are finding solutions to problems, writing a great short story or even a complete novel, you will find a market for that eBook if you follow the easy steps presented in this book.

You can always change content and edit your book. This means that you can keep adding and changing to meet your readers' needs. It is impossible to do that in a cost-effective way when you march down to your local bookstore and buy a printed and bound version. You will earn money as you perfect your eBook products and become a better writer. Did you ever think you would get a lifetime scholarship or grant to write books?

Let's get some of that scholarship or grant money right now!

This is truly a ***Cheap and Easy Guide to Self-publishing eBooks***. This book is laid out in such a way that each exercise builds upon the previous one. Begin at Chapter One and read the chapters in order. This is why you will be able to publish your first work to the world in just a few minutes after reading this book. You may have your first eBook published even before you are halfway through the book.

FAQ (Frequently Asked Questions Regarding Self-publishing eBooks)

1Q. Do I need to copyright my work?

1A. Yes, you should copyright your work. In the United States, where I live, copyright law automatically protects any document you create. The reason you file papers with the U.S Copyright Office is so that the U.S. government has a record of when, where and by whom this specific document was created.

2Q. Where do I go to copyright my work?

2A. Once you have completed your eBook, you can obtain the copyright forms from the United States Copyright Office on the Library of Congress Website. A "Cheap and Easy" way to getting the job done is by going to the United States Copyright Office located at:

http://www.loc.gov/copyright/

3Q. What is an ISBN number and do I need one?

3A. The ISBN number is a number that you will need for each binding of your eBook. For the two eBooks and marketing plans that I am including in this book, you can get by without an ISBN number. However, in order to present your eBook to traditional bookstores that will be selling eBooks, you will need an ISBN number. I will advise you how to get ISBN numbers later in the book. You can let your sales from publishing with the two basic publishing plans I offer pay for the cost of obtaining ISBN numbers.

Here is the address of RR Bowker, the company that issues the ISBN numbers. When applying for a number, always remember that even if you have just one book to publish, you will need many additional numbers.

For example, if you publish your book on a CD-ROM you will need a number. If you publish your eBook as a digital file to download off the Internet, you will need another ISBN number.

If you decide to publish the same book in printed form you need another number. You must have separate ISBN numbers for hardbound, softcover, trade paperback, audio books, and any other potential binding you can think of. You will need at least five ISBN numbers for every eBook you publish.

In order to make the eBook strategy work for you; consider publishing a series of three to five new books.

If you publish at least three versions or bindings on each book you will need at least 15 ISBN numbers to assign.

Read the specifications and directions at:

http://www.bowker.com/

4Q. How do I keep someone from stealing my eBook and passing it out to everyone for free?

4A. If a person wants to steal your material, what prevents him from buying your bound version from a local bookstore, ripping the pages out of the book, scanning the pages into his computer, and selling your brilliance? Theft can happen, but if you are making more money than you can spend and becoming very popular, maybe it will actually be a good thing for you in the final tally. After all, just recently Stephen King the great American author gave out free copies of his newest eBook over the Internet. Over 400000 people responded and overloaded the network servers of major Internet booksellers. Even if a few free copies were pirated, don't you think Stephen King benefited by the publicity associated with those kinds of sales figures?

5Q. Can I publish an eBook and then publish a bound version of the same book?

5A. Yes, you can! In fact you may find you have a much better product to sell as you receive feedback from people that have spent money on your eBook and basically perform a job of editing for you at the same time. Your success in publishing in this fashion will give you new insights and new markets to explore using traditional print publishers. Make sure you study each eBook-publishing contract. Some publishers will want exclusive rights to publish your work in electronic format. Some publishers will even ask for exclusive print rights. When you see the word "exclusive" in a contract, run away. Just because print publishers may have a handle on the print world, they may have no clue on how to reach the book buyers of the electronic world.

Electronic book publishers have no lock on the Internet buying market either. The eBook publishing business changes daily. You need to keep up with what is going on. You need to educate yourself and stay ahead of the curve. You can accomplish this feat by selling your eBooks through many different eBook sellers.

6Q. Can I include pictures or video in my eBooks?

6A. Yes, you can. However, it may be best to offer text only eBooks with links that take the reader to the Internet to view full color illustrations and video. If you keep the file size small by including just a few pictures, it will be easier to deliver to your buyers' e-mail. Generally you want to keep the file size under one megabyte so you can deliver your eBooks easily over the Internet. Hyperlinks also add to the size of the document. For example I have a 186-page eBook that is all text. The file size is 200k. When created hyperlinks and bookmarks from the table of contents to the chapter headings, the size of the document grew to 640k.

If you want to e-publish and want tons of graphics, links, sound and video then you need to purchase a CD Re-Writer. Good ones cost around $300.

Many CD-ROMs hold 600 megabytes of information. Reference books and mailing lists are published on CD-ROM.

7Q. How much money can I earn selling my eBooks?

7A. That is a hard question to answer. There is no guarantee that you will sell anything. However, if you use the techniques outlined in this book, your chances of earning book royalties are fantastic!

You will be more profitable at selling eBooks than many other Internet products.

Why? Because of the instant gratification and privacy it offers the reader and the wonderful value inherent associated with books.

8Q. How long does it take me to get my finished eBook uploaded and actually have it selling on the Internet?

8A. With some servers it may take a week or two, with other's including your own, it may take 15 minutes!

Yes, in 15 minutes you will start showing off your book to the entire world!

9Q. What subjects are hot right now?

9A. The best selling subjects right now seem to be how to, romance, erotica, health, and non-fiction.

Go to barnesandnoble.com and borders.com and look at the book titles they are marketing. This will give you a good idea of what is hot and what is not.

10Q. How can I sell my eBooks in traditional bookstores?

10A. Both Barnes & Noble and Borders are planning to sell eBooks out of their traditional stores. Amazon.com will be selling eBooks by the time this book is in printed form.

By the time mainstream book publishing gets involved selling eBooks, your popularity and sales figures may get the attention of store managers when the time comes to include eBooks in their business plans. Now, many independent storeowners sell eBooks in the form of floppy disks and CD-ROMs.

At this very moment, two of the major traditional book wholesalers, Ingram and Baker & Taylor are considering offering eBooks to their customers. Their customers include traditional bookstores and libraries.

11Q. Where Can I find eBooks?

11A. The cheap and easy way to get familiar with eBooks is to locate and read the many free eBooks located on-line. The largest resource is a website called Project Gutenberg, located at:

http://www.gutenberg.net

There you will find around 10,000 free eBooks. These will be easy to read because they are formatted in straight ASCII text, just like all of your e-mail messages. This way they can be easily downloaded on 99% of the computers in existence.

You will find eBooks that are in "public domain." This means that anyone can distribute these eBooks without worrying about violating copyright.

Another great source of free eBooks and book samplers is called the Rocket Library. It is located at:

http://www.rocket-library.com

You will be able to download and read these books in the new Rocketbook eBook format and you can contribute to the Rocketbook Library.

Since many eBook-publishing houses distribute their own free eBooks to the Rocketbook Library, your free eBook may get the attention of eBook publishers.

12Q. Where Can I purchase new eBooks?

12A. Here are some wonderful places to purchase eBooks.

1stbooks Library:

http://www.1stbooks.com

The Booklocker:

http://www.booklocker.com

Fatbrain:

http://www.fatbrain.com

Mightywords:

http://www.mightywords.com

Rocket Edition Books by NuvoMedia available at Barnes & Noble and Powells.com:

http://www.bn.com

http://www.powells.com

Softbook Editions by the Softbook Press:

http://www.softbook.com

Softlock:

http://www.softlock.com

The NetLibrary:

http://www.netlibrary.com

To get a more complete and up to date list, go to major search engine directories like Yahoo, altavista, excite, etc, and search on the words, "eBooks" or "electronic books."

Are you excited? The list gets bigger every day. Good luck! Your first eBook will soon be listed and sold by many of the above eBook sellers!

Summary:

There are many places located on the Internet to publish and sell your eBooks. At least once a week perform a search on the search directory Yahoo at:

http://www.yahoo.com

Search on the words, "eBooks" "ebooks" and "eBook publishers" The results will give you additional markets to sell your eBooks and give you many ideas on effective ways to market them.

You also learned how to get a copyright for your works and where to apply for an ISBN number.

Chapter Two

What Do I Gain by Publishing eBooks?

The economics of eBook publishing

The economics of publishing books in electronic form are too good to ignore. Today, you will find very few reference books that are published in a traditional fashion. CD-ROMs are manufactured in amazing numbers allowing families of all income levels access to information.

What are the economics of traditional book publishing?

Here is what a typical self-publisher is up against. In order to get book printing costs down to a bearable level, in other words in the $3 or $4 range, the self-published author will need a first run of books at around 3000 to 5000 copies. The cover art will cost at a minimum of $2500 for the first run. If you work the numbers, the self-published author has to spend at least $12000 in printing costs alone.

This is before the author has sold a solitary book!

After the author has spent the money he owns 3000 copies of the masterpiece.

How do the authors sell and deliver their books to the reader?

Most self-publishing marketing books will tell you that in order to sell the book; the author needs favorable reviews. The review process works like this:

The author sends out press releases to book reviewers representing the genre of the book. If the reviewer becomes interested in the press release, the author will receive a request for a "review copy."

The author digs into the stash of books, pulls out a copy, attaches a reviewer or a media kit, and pays for the postage. On a $5 book that may add another $5 in shipping materials as well as postage. Many reviewers will ask you to ship your books by overnight express. The author may find himself spending up to $18 - $25 per reviewer!

One reviewer in Berlin, Germany became very excited over my first book. He requested that I ship a review copy by airfreight, from Phoenix, Arizona in the United States to Berlin, Germany. It cost me around $75 to ship the book and review kit.

Guess what? I never received a review nor heard from the reviewer again!

Experts in the self-publishing field, state that you must send between 300-500 review copies to target genre reviewers before your book has a chance to become a hit. If you send out 500 book copies at a minimum of $10 per book, you have spent another $5000 of your money.

Now you have to market the book. It's your job as the self-published author to get the books into the store, and it is your job to move the books from the store to your customers.

Many self-publishing marketing experts feel it takes around $30000 per title to effectively market a book.

So here is the rundown of what it costs.

What it costs to print and sell a self-published book

$12000 to print and place a cover on your book.

$ 5000 to send books to reviewers

$30000 to market each book effectively.

$47000 is your total investment.

Out of your initial 3000 run of books you have already given away 500 leaving you with 2500 copies to sell.

Assuming your retail price is $20 per book and you can maintain that retail price for one year, the most you will bring in if you sell every remaining book is: $50000

If you subtract the $47000 you incurred as expenses you will have a net income of only $3000.

Believe me when I tell you that will be the hardest you have ever worked for only $3000.

Are these figures realistic? Yes, they are! Ask any self-published author what it cost to print and sell books.

Now let us use an example of creating or publishing an eBook and bringing it to market.

We will assume that you will want your own website. It is possible to sell eBooks without one, but lets look at all of the possibilities.

Let's assume that you have a computer and word processing software. You will need that anyway to self-publish your book the traditional way.

What it costs to publish and sell an eBook

What does it cost to publish and sell an eBook?

1. Cost of a Website with secure credit card ordering is $1200 per year. I am estimating on the high side here. You can spend less and have an effective website.

2. Cost of an Internet provider is $360 per year.

3. Adobe Acrobat Software is $269 (One time charge)

Create as many eBooks as you want with this software. Check out the Resources on my website and get the best price if you wish.

http://www.eBook-marketing.com

4. Marketing costs. You can get by using "sweat equity" in other words you don't need to spend anything. (You just saved **$30000** Congratulations!) I will explain "Finger Tip Marketing" later on.

5. Cover Graphics. You don't really need any unless you are posting to Amazon.com or barnesandnoble.com. There are people who will charge $500 or less to create an attractive eBook cover for you. Let's estimate on the high side of $500. You can use software like Paint Shop Pro or other graphic design software or take a picture, scan it into your computer and use that as your cover art.

6. Review Copies. There are eBook reviewers. You send the reviewers e-mail attachments that include copies of your eBook. Your cost to send it is **$0**. Think of how many reviewers you can service on the Internet. You will be happy to send out a review copies when you are not paying $10 or $20 per reviewer.

7. Once you own your eBook publishing software, the cost to "print" the eBook in digital form as an Adobe Acrobat, ASCII text, or as a Microsoft Word Document is **$0**.

Your total cost of the eBook production run of 3000 eBooks and your cost of sending these to 500 eBook reviewers including the total marketing costs for one year is

$1129. Now that you own the software for your next eBook projects, the total cost for each successive eBook is

$860.

If you sell that **$20** book for only **$10** as an eBook thus giving your reader 50% savings, you will bring in $30000 less $1129 or **$28871**.

Many on-line eBook sellers are selling eBooks at only a 20% discount compared to the printed and bound versions. If you follow that model you will receive **$48000** with out of pocket expense of only $1129.

I am assuming a print run of 3000 eBooks in this example. An eBook is a digital file. If you have orders for **10000000** copies for the year, the cost will still remain at $1129 for the first year!

Do you see why this may be the best time in your life to consider finishing that novel or to begin selling eBooks and booklets on-line?

Now is the best time your eBooks will stand out in a small crowd. In just a few years the situation may change. It may actually become harder to break into the publishing business. Everyone will be in it and your eBooks may become harder to differentiate from your competition. Acting now and acting fast will get you way ahead of the learning curve. It will also guarantee that you will participate in those amazing profits.

On Tuesday, March 14, 2000 Stephen King released his book *Riding the Bullet.* This short story was only released as an eBook. He released it as a RocketEdition from NuvoMedia, and as Adobe Acrobat digital files from Softlock and as a download to a Palm Pilot formatted and distributed by the Peanut Press. There were over **400000** orders for Stephen's eBook, worldwide in just one day!

400000 orders for a book for an entire year would be fantastic. It cost just as much to produce one copy as it does to print **400000**. You have that capability through selling your eBooks off of your own site and off of sites hosted by others.

Once eBooks get into the mainstream of Bookselling, the numbers should really go off the charts!

Are you ready to include yours?

So do you feel good about the prospects? I do. One of my eBooks, *How To Hypnotize People and Other Living Things,* is outselling my first book, *How To Hypnotize Yourself Without Losing Your Mind* even though my first book is selling in traditional brick and mortar stores and is on just about every internet bookstore.

Someday I may release *How to Hypnotize People and Other Living Things* as a softcover paper bound book, but I am in no hurry. I love the returns from selling eBooks.

Are you ready? Lets go ahead an publish our first eBook and market it over the Internet!

Creating your first eBook

Authors tend to be perfectionists. Once you have completed your work and look at it, you realize that changes could have been made to make a much better product.

That is the best part of creating eBooks. You can publish and sell your first draft, capture the names and addresses of your customers, publish a second draft, contact your customers by e-mail or give them the updated eBook at no cost. (You can always have them subscribe to updates of your eBook files for a fee) You can perfect your eBook and give your e-customers, a wonderful product that grows and expands.

You can market your books or complementary books and products to your customer base. You will develop relationships with your readers. Isn't it ironic that with the mass appeal of the Internet the author can actually hand sell titles to readers anywhere in the world?

The economics of publishing eBooks is too good to ignore. Now is your chance to become a published author. This is the most exciting time in human history.

Right now there is an engineer from Bangalore, India, an architect from Malta, a nurse from Hong Kong, a construction worker from Sweden, an automobile worker from Germany, a homemaker from Salt Lake City, and a school teacher from Italy, who want to read your eBook!

Act now and feed the world with your creativity and mark the world with your brilliance!

Summary:

Chapter Two discussed statistics related to traditional book publishing and eBook publishing. The numbers speak for themselves.

In order to guarantee a profit in the book publishing industry, you must create and sell eBooks effectively.

The economics of eBook publishing makes sense.

You will save money on production costs.

You will realize a higher rate of return with eBook publishing than standard book publishing.

You will be able to perfect your eBook by making changes to the text whenever you feel it necessary.

Chapter Three

How to Publish Your eBook in One Day

Now you are going to learn my 5-Step method in publishing your first eBook.

Here is my quick 5-Step Method of publishing **your first eBook.** You will publish your first eBook within a few hours of reading this chapter.

Does this sound exciting? I think so. Let us begin!

Step One: Create a document on your computer. How big should the document be? Lets start out with 5-25 pages.

The document could be one of your best speeches, a food recipe, a short story or a step by step instruction like a "how to book" with behavioral objectives in mind.

My top selling eBook **titled *How To Hypnotize People and Other Living Things***, for example, is only 36 pages long but outsells my 193 page eBook by a 3 to 1 ratio! People want concise and useful information and they want it delivered quickly.

Step Two: Save your document as a Microsoft Word document, an ASCII text tile, or an Adobe Acrobat PDF file.

Step Three: Connect to the Internet and go to Mightywords.com at http://www.mightywords.com.

Step Four: Follow Mighty Word's directions about adding pricing and commentary. Check out their on-line eBook store to get an idea of what categories your eBook may fit. You will be assigned a password and you can always edit the eBook content at any time. Mighty Words.com will also ask you where to send your *quarterly royalties*.

There is a very small charge for storage of your eBooks on Mighty Word's server.

Step Five: Now think about how you will spend your new revenue steam. Breathe deeply...now find more on-line eBook sellers that want you to publish on their websites!

Congratulations! You are now an official eBook author.

Summary:

Publishing on Mightywords.com will be the cheapest and easiest solution in posting and selling your first eBook on the Internet. Is your work done?

No, your work has just begun. You need to proceed on and learn Internet marketing techniques that are guaranteed to bring you success.

Each marketing technique will be free of charge. These techniques will allow you to "let your fingers do the selling!"

Chapter Four

Marketing Your First eBook with No Budget

Using Fingertip Marketing to Sell Your Books

Q: What is Fingertip Marketing?

A: Fingertip Marketing is defined as, any marketing that adheres to the following two requirements:

1. It is free of charge.

2. It includes no verbal sales pitch to anyone.

>   You communicate through your computer keyboard using your fingertips.

Q: How did you come up with Fingertip Marketing as an effective way to sell eBooks?

I actually believed that I would be in a universal listing that bookstore managers and librarians would see and then order my book.

Boy, was I stupid!

The truth is that the author must do all of the marketing of his/her book.

There is no universal listing that will get libraries and bookstores to order your books.

You have to become a "salesperson."

Most authors that I have met are not salespeople. In fact many authors I meet despise salespeople.

The Insurance Sales professional

Think about how the typical insurance sales professional works each and every day.

The insurance salesperson has to call on people called "suspects" of which many are not interested in his/her product. Most people will not be interested in buying insurance.

From the group of "suspects" evolves a smaller group called "prospects." Prospects are people who are interested in buying insurance.

Out of that smaller group called "prospects" evolves "customers" or the people that actually purchase the insurance policies.

The next day the salesperson gets up in the morning and begins the procedure all over again. Every day is exactly the same as the day before.

Does this sound like fun? It can be a great deal of fun. But most authors I meet would never be comfortable working in an environment like that.

Characteristics of the insurance sales job.

Many insurance sales professionals work eight to twelve hours a day, five days per week. However, they must meet with they're clients when the clients are ready. Many successful insurance professionals spend weekends selling insurance.

Insurance salespeople are usually restricted to handling specific insurance products and they are restricted to a specific geographical territory.

The Traditional Book Author

Here is the typical day of a book author once the book is published.

The author makes a list of bookstores, contacts the Bookstore Manager or the Community Relations Coordinator, if it is a chain bookstore.

The author then makes a sales presentation to interest the store in carrying the book.

The author will try to schedule a book-signing event or just get the bookstore to place a purchase order for books right away.

The bookstores are called "suspects."

Most bookstores already have enough books on their shelves so the author has to employ super sales skills in winning over the bookstore decision-maker to buy books or schedule a book signing.

If the store agrees to purchase the book, the decision-maker will tell the author that they will only deal through an established book wholesaler. They do not purchase books from individual authors.

The author must call the book wholesalers or large distributors and sell the wholesalers or distributors in carrying his/her book.

Excellent sales skills are needed for this process.

Several follow-up sales calls are made by the author and hopefully the wholesaler or distributor will agree to carry the book.

Now, the author will go back to the bookstore and offer to present a book-signing event.

The bookstore CRC will jump for joy to get the author signing booked for that day.

Author signing events are usually booked up eight weeks in advance to make sure there will be books available to sell.

The bookstore orders 40 books from the author's wholesaler. The books will not be paid for until after the completion of the book-signing event.

The author goes to Kinkos or some other office print shop and creates banners, bookmarks, and other marketing materials. The author pays for the materials.

The author calls radio stations, writes news releases and calls personal friends to attend the book-signing event.

The book signing is held. Fifty or sixty people show up to listen to the author.

Five people purchase books.

Immediately, after the book signing the bookstore sends the remaining 35 books back to the publisher.

Thirty days after the book signing the author goes to the bookstore and asks for payment for the five books sold a month before.

The bookstore requests the author to invoice the store at this time. The publisher will receive payment and the author receive a royalty check for those five books purchased from the wholesaler within 90 days of the book-signing event.

Any unsold books that were returned in damaged condition will be credited against royalty payments.

Returns can run between 7% and 35%!

Does this sound like fun to you? How much money does it cost you and how much time will you spend selling five books at a signing?

This is a very realistic example of booksignings. In fact, if the author sells five books at the event the store considers it a success! You have introduced many people that will purchase other books while they are in the store or at a later date.

If you were to present this book-signing example to successful insurance sales professionals that are earning over $100000 per year, they will simply not believe you!

The author spends too much time selling for too little money.

The eBook Author

The eBook author writes a book.

The eBook author posts books on Mightywords.com.

An hour later the book is selling over the Internet. Mightywords is handling payment and fulfillment of each order.

There are no book returns.

Then the author posts the book to other eBook selling websites, negotiating all contracts by e-mail. The author never has to speak to another individual and waste valuable time over the telephone.

The author takes a sample chapter or an article and submits this information to top websites that may be interested in the author's subject area.

Offering content for web visitors greatly enhances the value of the already popular websites. Almost all of the website content managers will jump for the opportunity to give their web visitors more reasons to come back to their websites.

The sample chapters and articles are given in exchange for links back to the author's book listing at Mightywords.com, the Booklocker, 1stbooks Library, or perhaps the author's own website.

If you can propose just four or five new article postings each day for just five days per week, you can achieve tremendous success in selling your eBooks.

This is a great technique used by authors that have to work a regular job for a living. The authors can create and deliver their proposals by e-mail. They don't have to make business contacts during working hours. By working just a few hours each night and on weekends, each author can drive thousands of readers to his own website within just a few months.

Once the article is posted to a website it will stay in a particular location for a while and then will be "archived" for new subscribers to read later on.

The article will include links back to the author's website or a designated book selling website and will be referenced by major search engines.

This gives the author a major boost in popularity.

A great benefit of this type of selling for an author is the fact that no words are spoken. No sales skills are needed.

If the eBook author prices the book at only $10 per book and each contact for the month sells one book per contact, the author will sell over $1000 in volume the very first month of book selling!

The author will receive anywhere from 25% to 100% of the sales totals based on the arrangements made with eBook sellers and eBook publishers.

For this example let us assume that the author earns $500 clear profit for the first month of selling eBooks.

How much did the author have to spend in marketing the eBook?

Zero!

The author did not have to make banners, bookmarks or other marketing materials.

The author did not have to make a single phone call.

In the second month, if the author executes the same marketing strategy, another 100 eBook sellers or book referring websites will be added to the author's sales force.

Again, if each eBook publisher only sells one book, the author has $500 plus another $500 from the original websites that are selling or referring his book from their archived web locations.

If the author keeps up this pace and the book selling websites are only sending one new book buyer each month, the author will keep $39000 the first year.

If the author adds a second book, the total could be $78000 or more.

Also, remember the author will receive around 100% of what is selling from his own website.

We are not factoring in you working more than two or three hours per day. We are not factoring in the fact that you can set up an affiliate program like Amazon.com or Barnes & Noble and bring potentially thousands of potential book-sellers to link over to your website and send you business.

The example is based on each of your website content contacts. Each of the contacts has your sample chapter or article sending you just one customer each month!

You are adding hundreds of sales people each month that are working 24 hours per day, 7 days per week. There are no product or territory restrictions.

You may wish to go back and send each contact two or three articles thus doubling or tripling your eBook sales.

You still haven't spent any money!

Show this model to insurance sales professionals.

Watch how huge their eyes become when they listen to your eBook-marketing plan!

Q: Can I sell my very first eBook without spending any money?

A: Yes. Actually you will have to pay a small amount of money for eBook storage charges but the fee is only $1 per month at Mightywords.com.

Let's begin by showing you how to take care of marketing your eBook on Mightywords.com

After you sign up you will receive confirmation e-mail and the URL (universal resource locator) of each eBook you upload. Once you have that URL or Internet address of your eBook, consider that a website. In order to sell your eBook you must market the eBook effectively yourself.

You will be put in the Mightywords.com website so people can find you but just as you are listed in a traditional bookstore with a traditional bound book, it is still up to the author to push the book.

Fortunately, you don't have to spend any money to accomplish this goal. The magic about using the Internet for marketing is that you always have two choices to make. You can pay for marketing or you can get it for free.

It may cost money to get featured on Amazon.com or barneandnoble.com. When you enter a brick and mortar bookstore and see books facing out on a table, the publisher and sometimes the author paid for that placement. Book placement in a retail store just isn't a whim of the store manager or the favorite employee's choice. You spend money to get the best position in the stores.

By marketing your eBooks over the Internet, you will always have a choice to pay or not to pay. Elect not to pay. Once you have extinguished all of the free marketing resources then make a decision to pay. You may surprise yourself and really find some great things that work for you without spending a dime for marketing expenses.

I am betting you never run out of effective free Internet resources.

It is absolutely impossible to run out of free Internet marketing opportunities.

This affiliate program is great. Rather than creating a space on your personal website you get to create your own personal eBook Store, which is stored on Fatbrain.com's server. You receive an Internet URL that you can link to your site or send to friends and insert in your marketing information. You can give your own special name to that store. Every time someone uses your unique eBook store to purchase eBooks, Mightywords pays you commissions.

You can earn up to 20% of the selling price at this writing. Even if you don't sell any of your eBooks through this linking process you may earn money on selling other "favorites" that are sold from your web links.

3. Contact discussion lists on the Internet and offer a free chapter of your eBook to the list manager. Copy and paste the sample chapter of your eBook and send this to the list manager. This is an effective technique I personally learned from Angela Adair-Hoy the author of *How to Write, Publish and Sell eBooks*. (Buy it, Angela has great information) You can find the URLs of the discussion lists in Chapter Seven of this book and on my website.

At the end of the sample chapter insert the precise link to your eBook located on Mightywords.com or the precise links to your Mightywords website store, or both. Make sure you insert the full URL with "http" included. This way a person can open the URLs by clicking on your text e-mail.

4. Conduct a search on Yahoo, the famous search directory. Look up the topic area of your eBook. Put yourself in your reader's shoes. What kind of information would they be looking for that your book is a perfect fit?

For example, if you have written a Southwestern Style Cookbook, who would be interested? Would people that are vacationing to Arizona or New Mexico be interested in southwestern style cooking? These people may be interested in Cowboy Poetry, or travel information.

Lets assume they enter search words like, *cooking* then Arizona or *New Mexico*. Your job is to search using the same words. Take the first 10 search returns and send an offer to the webmasters at each website. Offer to send t webmasters free articles or free chapters that will be posted on the websites. Top websites usually offer free content to their visitors. In exchange for posting your free chapter, tell the webmasters you will provide content with the consideration that you receive a bi-line that tells webs visitors where they can purchase your eBooks. Most webmasters will respond favorably to your offer.

5. Look up e-zines that fit your eBook genre. An e-zine is a newsletter that all the great websites offer to their visitors. E-zine editors are ALWAYS looking for articles.

E-mail a proposal to the e-zine editor and offer to submit an article or free chapter of your eBook.

You may even offer the e-zine editor non-exclusive serial rights to post a chapter for each issue in exchange for an advertisement in the e-zine.

You will offer the free information in exchange for links to your eBook store or your unique eBook Internet URL.

6. Contact your local newspaper and give them a similar offer.

7. Contact the editors of association newsletters that focus on your subject area. Make the newsletter editors the same offer. Association members have computers. They have the ability to purchase and read your eBooks.

8. Ask about speaking to the group on your topic. In exchange for speaking have handouts ready that include complete ordering instructions on how each member can order your eBook from Mightywords and other eBook order fulfilling websites.

9. Offer to teach a class based on your eBook at a community college. Make your eBook the required textbook. Print it out and put it into a binder. Set a price and get it into the college bookstore.

10. Read everything you can on marketing books and eBooks over the Internet. Create a marketing plan and do at least 3 eBook marketing activities each day.

Always believe in yourself. Your efforts will pay off with persistence. As you talk to other people about your newly published eBook, your friends, co-workers and relatives will give you valuable insights on other free eBook selling opportunities.

Summary:

You learned some of the basics of eBook Internet marketing. The same techniques may be used to market your traditionally bound books and other products as well.

Learning the secrets of Internet Marketing will enable you to out-perform many traditional Internet marketers.

I prefer fingertip marketing. Two features characterize fingertip marketing.

1. You never sell anyone using your voice.

2. You do not spend your money on advertising.

Chapter Five

What You Need To Sell eBooks From Your Website

Advantages of Selling from Your Website

1. You get to improve your daily business cash flow. The Booklocker for example, pays royalties every month. When you receive royalties from Mightywords and most of the other eBook sellers, you usually get paid quarterly. Some eBook sellers only pay you semiannually. I like instant gratification, don't you?

After all, that is why your readers are downloading your eBooks. They want instant gratification, too. By having your credit card processor deposit money into your business bank account every day, you get instant gratification with each and every sale. This is a great motivator.

2. Your personal website allows you to collect address information of each customer. Once you sell your customer their first eBooks, they are more apt to purchase more eBooks. You collect their e-mail addresses and send them updates. If you are a public speaker as well as an author, you can invite them to hear you speak when you are in their area. You are a celebrity.

3. Collecting data on which kinds of eBooks are of interest to your website visitors will increase your income. I found that by tracking my page hits, I could find out what information my web visitors were interested in and what kinds of eBooks they would actually purchase.

You can set up on-line forms, messages boards, and forums that allow your visitors many reasons to go back to your website. As your web visitors develop confidence in you, they will be more encouraged in placing orders with you.

4. You can offer free updates and information to your readers and distribute that information inexpensively with a website. Having a website is a very low cost proposition. I spend less than $100.00 per month when I include my website costs as well as having two different credit card processors. (I will explain more in Chapter Six: Setting Up Back-up Systems)

When I had an office in Scottsdale, Arizona my costs were almost $1200.00 per month. Now I get so much more for 10 % of what I use to pay and never have to leave my home.

5. You can set up "secret" places on your site that you charge a subscription fee for people to enter. You can have levels of newsletters for example. You can send out a free one and offer a more advanced newsletter or content site on your website that give the reader a great deal more.

You can set up this area to be password protected. Once the reader pays you the subscription fee, permission is granted to enter and download your unique information.

6. Offer free classes and fee classes to your readers. This is a variation of the above point number five. Free classes will allow the reader to get to know your style. Web visitors will be more apt to buy from you or take additional on-line classes, training or telephone consulting.

7. You can offer virtually unlimited text and graphics in describing your eBooks. You can record your voice and give author readings from your website. Many times I have found that the author reading was the key factor in getting the eBook sale.

8. You Can Realize A Greater Return on Investment. Even during the best of economic times, no one eBook seller or eBook publisher will be able to reach all of the eBook buying markets. When you offer eBook selling from your site you get instant feedback on what is working and what is not. You can experiment with offering "specials" that will instantly affect your bottom line sales and profits. Even though operating your own site can be a great deal of work, you can sell a ton of eBooks and keep a bigger chunk of each and every sale.

9. You can react quicker in the Market Place. For example, let's say a new company called YouandI eBooks comes out with a new software program that compresses video, sound files, and graphics in such a way that your file size never gets over 200k. That will allow you to create eBooks that are full multi-media productions. File size will not be an issue. You will be able to instantly offer a tremendous product to your all of your readers. Maybe the other booksellers and eBook publishers that are selling your eBook have no interest in formatting and using that product. So you can generate a large number of sales by offering it through your newsletters and your website.

I personally sell more eBooks from my site than any combination of all of the other eBook sellers I use put together. People want to obtain their material right from the source if they can. You are the source.

10. You can offer your own affiliate program. With your own website you can offer your own sales affiliate program. Affiliate programs are the reason why Amazon.com and barnesandnoble.com do so well selling on the Internet. For more information about offering Affiliate Programs, go to:

http://clickxchange.com/

http://www.linkshare.com/

You may purchase Affiliate Program Tracking Software to start your own affiliate program, track purchases and pay commissions by browsing to Marketingtips.com.

http://www.marketingtips.com

11. Join an existing Affiliate Program. You may want to associate with other big names and other authors by joining sales associate and affiliate programs like Barnes & Noble.com and Amazon.com. Visitors see major booksellers' logos and search engines on your website and overcome their fear of ordering from you when they notice brands they are familiar with. It appears that the bookstores are endorsing you! You can feature authors and books that are similar to yours. If someone purchases those books and you have an affiliation agreement set up with an Internet bookseller, you will receive a commission.

Even if you do not want to create the links back to Amazon.com or Barnes & Noble.com, join their programs anyway. There are Internet Marketing techniques that they share with affiliates that will be located on the corresponding affiliate program pages.

This information is very valuable. You will find links to other places you can post your eBooks as well.

Where do I purchase my website?

Ask people you know who are happy with their websites.

What do I look for when I purchase my own website?

The following are features you want to insure a great eBook selling website:

1. Toll free technical support. You need this because problems will happen. Its best to get 24/hour 7 day per week toll free service.

2. You need your own domain. A domain is a name you pick like freetosell.com or huas.net. Pick one that is simple for your readers to remember. The shorter the better. For example, barnesandnoble.com added the following domain names to their Internet bookseller. They added "bn.com" and "books.com"

3. E-mail boxes. These are unique e-mail addresses that will have your domain name as the home address. For example: f2s@ huas.net or anythingIwanttowrite@huas.net

4. You want a large number of Autoresponders. Autoresponders are one of the oldest and by far the best marketing tools you can have regardless of what Internet product or service you offer.

Autoresponders work like fax-on-demand systems. Visitors go to your website and notice that they can receive a free chapter of your eBook by clicking on a link. When the visitor clicks on the link, a e-mail software client opens with visitor's address as the recipient and your e-mail address as the sender.

The visitor clicks "send" in the e-mail client and in a minute a free chapter is sent to the visitor's inbox.

This is much faster then air delivery. The autoresponder document is delivered with lightning speed. You can load a sample chapter of your book along with complete ordering instructions. You can deliver your newsletters, press kit, articles, or just about any other text information very quickly. You do not have to be present when your reader requests the information.

My host, Valueweb gives me *unlimited* autoresponders for one monthly charge.

5. You want to be able to access daily statistics. You need to track how many web page views. You need to know the number of visitors you receive daily, weekly, and monthly. I know hosting services that don't allow you to receive daily statistics. Make sure you ask for this feature before you contract for a web hosting service.

6. You want to be able to administer your website, such as checking daily statistics and changing individual pages from any computer in the world. While you are at the Writer's Conference in Maui learning more about your craft or lying on the Maui beaches, celebrating your good fortune, you may want to check your new orders or add some new products. Make sure your web host allows you access to statistics. Offering a "hit counter" is not enough. You should have very detailed web statistics.

7. You want T-3 line connections by your website host to your website. T-3 lines are fast data transmission lines. Most hosts now use T-3's.

8. Microsoft FrontPage Extensions support. If you author your Website in Microsoft FrontPage , the extensions will allow you to create interactive forms. Now your website visitors can answer questions on line and give you immediate feedback and marketing information.

9. You want 100MB of storage. I have around a thousand pages on my website and don't come near that 100MB limit. However, when you add sound files, (your author interview or readings on-line) book covers, and video down the road, you may find that you really do need that much storage. Get more than you need now and you will grow into it.

10. You need support for e-commerce. Many websites now will make provisions for adding on your own store. A store is basically an order button or a shopping cart system that provides for a secured access page on your site.

You will still have to apply for your own Merchant Account or a Merchant account processor. I have more information about that and direct links to those sites located in Chapter Seven.

How do I design my website?

Look at other sites that sell eBooks. Check out their index pages. Index pages are the default pages you view when you enter the URL into your browser. Find a site that loads quickly and you can read the information clearly. You may want to copy that design.

A good index page or home page should load at 4.6 seconds at 28.8 speed. Additional pages on the site should be smaller than 40k in size.

Most of my pages are 10k or less in size.

Do I have to learn HTML in order to have a website?

Yes, you will need to know some HTML. You can purchase an HTML editor program like Microsoft's FrontPage. Look for an editor that claims it is a WYSIWYG editor.

WYSIWYG is an acronym for *what you see is what you get.* FrontPage looks like Microsoft Word. It will have the same menus and page set up.

As you are typing in the content of your page, HTML is created underneath the document. There is a tab you can select and you can view the HTML and make changes. I would recommend a WYSIWYG HTML editor program to begin your website project.

Learn how to create links in HTML and to create "Bold" and "Italics" text. You need to know how to create paragraphs. You will need this skill when you are adding eBook commentary to Amazon.com and Barnes & Noble.com.

I have a nephew who is a website designer. Should I use him?

I would only use him if he will sit you down and teach you what he knows about web design. Web design can make your site look pretty, or web design can be profitable. Most sites opt to look pretty and most of these millions of websites on the Internet make absolutely ***no money at all.***

A web designer is interested in making the site look great. Most designers don't have a clue as far as how to bring people to your site and purchase your products.

Also, many times I hear Internet marketing consultants say, "if you don't want to spend money designing a site, have your 15 year old kid do it."

Well, if your 15-year-old kid is the top salesman for Realty Executives, Nationwide Insurance, or Johnson and Johnson Medical Products, than yes, I would agree.

Internet website design is all about SALES and very little about design. Remember that 99.9% of all business sites are losing money by having their own website. These are websites that are usually professionally designed by an official web designer.

You can do a great deal better by learning sound Internet marketing techniques and applying those techniques with a simple web design.

What do I need to bring lots of visitors to my site?

The following seven elements are necessary for you to bring visitors to your site.

1. A fast loading home page. It should load at 4.6 seconds with a 28.8bps modem. If you design your home pages and view it with a 56K modem or a cable modem, you will be not be looking at what most of your paying customers are looking at.

Speed decreases over distance due to many technical issues but the one thing to remember is, design your speed to the lowest modem speed available.

Keep away from black backgrounds. The color black is a composite of all of the colors of the rainbow. When someone selects a black background every single pixel or picture cell on your monitor has to be painted, with every single color available.

This takes time. Look at search engine websites. They all have white backgrounds. White, being the absence of all color will help your page load quickly.

Don't put any photographs or banners on your home page or index pages. If you must have them, place them on separate pages and link them with a text link to your index or home page.

Keep all of the text on your index page above the "scroll line." Only 30 % of your viewers will look below the scroll line on an index page.

2. Create "Meta tags" for your index pages and all of the pages you create on your site. There is a free website listed that will make Meta tags for your site and send them back to you through your e-mail. Meta tags include information about your site that is classified and used by search engines when people conduct keyword Internet searches.

Here is a brief course: Click on the following website.

http://www.wayneperkins.net

When you are there, look at your tool bar at the top of your browser and look for VIEW. Then click on VIEW, and PAGE SOURCE, or it may say SOURCE or HTML.

You may want to print this out. You are printing the "PAGE SOURCE" or the HTML.

Now lets look at the META tags.

You will find the following html text near the top of the page.

<head>

\<title\>Hypnotism Education: How To Hypnotize Yourself On The Internet, Wayne F. Perkins,

Hypnotherapist\</title\>

\<meta NAME="keywords" CONTENT="how to hypnotize,hypnosis,hypnosis bookstore,self-hypnosis, autogenics,books,eBooks,instruction, training, hypnotism forum,fear,phobia, hypnotist,autogenics, bookstore,eBooks,hypnotherapist,digital books,virtual books, rocketbook,softbook, Wayne Perkins"\>

\<meta NAME="description"CONTENT="Hypnotism Education is a site created by Wayne Perkins,Hypnotherapist Free self-hypnosis training and hypnosis scripts for students,largest hypnosis bookstore."\>

\</head\>

Between the \<head\> and \</head\> html tags you will see the \<title\> \</title\> html tags.

Just below title but still within the \<head\> element of the home page you will see a Meta tag called \<keywords\> and one called \<description\> and one called \<classification\>

If you are writing a mystery eBook. Your Meta tags will look something like this:

\<Head\>

\<Meta name="description" content="this is a mystery story eBook by author John Doe that takes place in the Western United States in 1880 titled The Strange Cowboy Murder"\>

\<meta name="keywords" content="mystery book, eBook, western united states, The Strange Cowboy Murder, 1880 Western America, John Doe, author, cowboys, western lore, stories"\>

\</head\>

NOTE: Use the format with all of the quotation marks and < signs exactly how I placed them. You can use either upper case or lower case lettering in your \<tags\> Use both upper and lower case in your \<key words\> and \<description\> tags.

The end of the \<description\> tag always ends with "\>

Search engines and directories many times look for these tags in classifying their sites. No tags, no classification.

Now you are going to learn the <keywords> tag. At the end of the keywords tag it will always end with ">

You may have up to 1500 characters in your keywords.

Notice in my example I have several words or phrases separated by commas. Your keywords are anything that appears between those commas, A key word can be a single word or a series of words. Do not use the same word more than 3 times in your keyword section. Search engines may dump them out. They call it, "spamming the page."

After you are finished with the <keywords> and <description> tags, you can end the whole series, with the </head> tag. This means you have finished the <head> section of the home page or index page.

If you have several pages on your site, each one should have its own <description> and <keywords> tags. Search engines will now find more ways for people to find you.

Your name and book title should be included in the <keywords> tag and the <description> tag.

You can find additional Meta tag instruction at:

http://www.searchenginewatch.com

3. Start A Free Newsletter. You need a free newsletter to give your visitors a reason to come back often to your website. When your readers subscribe to your newsletter you can include national or international updates in your field, advertising about your eBooks and other interesting information about your eBook genre.

Free newsletters are a great way to obtain repeat buyers. There are websites that will "host" your free newsletter. Some are listed in Chapter Seven.

If you are too busy to create your own newsletter, make an agreement with another webmaster to place a subscription button on your website, in exchange for a link back to yours or free advertising in his newsletter. You will be giving your readers more content and the other webmaster more people interested in visiting his site.

4. Begin and maintain an ongoing link exchange program. Your site will not be popular right away. Most websites only get 50 or 60 hits a month in the beginning. Every time you go and look at your site, that counts as a hit. So if you look at your own website once or twice a day, you have accounted for your 50 or 60 hits per month. One way to begin with a bang is to start a link exchange program.

Begin by searching for free information that applies to your book's subject or genre. Search on Yahoo and other major search engines. When the top 10 search returns come up, send e-mail to the webmasters at each of the websites listed and ask if they would like to add sample chapters of your eBook to offer their readers on line.

In return you need to include the URL of your website, or the specific link to your eBook on Mightywords, 1stbooks Library, the Booklocker, or Barnes & Noble.

The order URL on your website and on Mightywords.com will experience a rapid increase in the amount of hits. You will benefit by getting orders. It is easier to get your information published on other high visibility websites than it is to lure everyone over to your website.

Every week conduct additional searches on keywords that you feel other people would use that are interested in your subject and send more content offers to other websites.

You may even offer to publish your eBooks in serial form.

Serial form means that the other websites receive sample chapters each month in return for links to ordering information on your website.

Readers get your eBook little by little. If it looks good, readers will purchase right away rather than to have to wait several months to read the entire book for free.

This is one of the most profitable ways of using your time on the Internet. You won't have to spend any money on marketing if you keep up this program. You will help websites stay up high on the search return list of major search engines, and the people that do arrive on your site are there for one purpose...to purchase your eBooks!

5. **Offer credit card processing for your orders.** Without credit card processing, you won't survive. You can either obtain merchant status with a merchant account or you can have a merchant account processor do the work for you. I actually use both. I love the merchant account processor that processes on-line and in real-time. You don't need to send them any financial information and you are accepted immediately. CCSLIDE is located at:

http://www.ccslide.com

They are included in Chapter Seven of this book.

Also, you will want to sign up with as many eBook resellers to offer your eBooks as you can find. They will reach markets that you may never find. They will also accept credit cards and perform the entire order fulfillment for your customers.

6. **Autoresponders are a requirement!** You need autoresponders for your site. Each autoresponder can contain an eBook chapter and ordering information. If you want to see how they work send e-mail to:

autoresp@wayneperkins.net

You will now experience the advantage of using autoresponders.

The e-mail will arrive in your e-mail box within a few minutes. My website host, Valueweb provides me with 500 separate autoresponders for free when I pay them my $19.95 per month for my website-hosting fee.

You can also find free autoresponder host sites that will give you autoresponders even if you have no website. Now that your first eBook is finished, you should sign up for free autoresponders and start giving webmasters the autoresponder addresses so you can deliver free chapters of your eBook. I will list some free autoresponders sites in Chapter Seven.

7. Study and implement website changes every week. Search engines know which websites are changing content on a regular basis. Websites are not static telephone book advertising. The more often you change your site, the higher your site will be mentioned in the search returns for that topic and that is what will make your site popular. Most corporate websites change very little or not at all.

Corporate directors usually don't realize that a website is a function of sales, marketing and customer service.

Since websites have something to do with computers, most corporate directors dump the job in the hands of the IS Department rather then the Sales, Marketing and Customer Service departments.

This may explain why corporate websites perform poorly and are a major disappointment.

Summary:

You have begun your journey into setting up your own website. You learned how to create Meta tags. Meta tags enable search engines and Internet directories to find you very quickly. They help you get positioned higher in the search engine results.

You learned what to look for when selecting a website hosting service to deliver your information to the world.

You also learned some website strategies that will help you achieve success.

Learning Internet Website design secrets will go far in stacking the cards in your favor so you become successful in selling eBooks.

Chapter Six

Setting Up Back-up Systems

What is a back up system and why do I need to set one up?

A back up system is a system of backing up all of your website, autoresponder and credit card processing information.

A back up system is needed because sooner or later, your computer system will fail, your website will go down or your credit card processor will have problems preventing your customers in placing orders.

Sometimes two or three of these events will happen at the same time. A back up system is necessary to keep the flow of money going into your bank account and keeping your visitors and customers happy.

You also need to back up your computer each night.

A few weeks before I started this book, I had my primary credit card processor go down for a two-week period.

Within a half-hour I had changed the buying links on my pages to activate my secondary account processor. It was a lifesaver. I received over 100 orders or $1000 in that period that I would have lost forever.

People want immediate gratification when ordering eBooks. They will move on and purchase your competitors' books if they find a problem on your website.

Here are some "Cheap and Easy" ways of insuring an effective back up system.

1. Credit card processing. Always remember that people want to order on-line and in real time. They want immediate credit card fulfillment. If you only have one credit card processor then, mention in a customer service area of your website or somewhere on the ordering page, that if there is a problem to "click here to order." The link they are clicking on will take them to your eBook description on Mightywords, the Booklocker or the 1stbooks Library eBook Stores.

When they reach the store, web visitors will be able to purchase all of your eBook titles because you will have already uploaded eBooks from the information you learned in Chapter Three.

Make it very easy for your customers to purchase your eBooks even if your systems go down.

2. Give your customers an opportunity to order by phone, fax or e-mail. Some people never will trust posting their credit card on-line. They will however give their credit card information to a disembodied voice or fax it to a strange, long distance number. Give your customers that option.

Install voice mail on your telephone and make it clear that your customers can leave a detailed message complete with name as it appears on the card, the credit card number, expiration date, and the item that they wish to order.

Out of every 500 or 600 orders, I will get a phone call for help or to place an order. Most problems are solved however through the effective use of e-mail.

3. Computer systems for file back up. Compact disc re-writers are the rage for backing up computer systems.

Good ones cost less than $300.00. When you hear people talk about burning in CD's, that's what they are talking about.

You can back up all of your files on CD-ROMs and then store them in another room. If you burn up a hard disk or lose information that includes your website pages, you can easily restore all of the information from your CD-ROMs.

Get in a habit of restoring your computer every time you make a change on your website. You can back up the text files that you are using for your autoresponders the same way.

Of course you have autoresponder text stored on you hosting website, but if the information becomes corrupt or lost, you can easily restore from your back up CD-ROMs.

Now, with the low prices, of CD-ROM Re-writers, you will not only have a great way of backing up your files, but also a new version of a printing press to create CD-ROM eBook titles.

At this point in time, Amazon.com does not allow you to sell eBooks from their catalog as downloaded files.

However, if you have published CD-ROM versions of your eBooks and have valid ISBN numbers assigned, you can include them in Amazon.com's on-line book catalog.

You may add book reviews and commentary just like the big-time publishers. You can even get Amazon.com to stock your CD-ROM's in their "Advantage" program.

For details on the Advantage Program go to:

http://www.amazon.com/advantage

You may use your new CD-ROM Re-writer as your in-house printing press. You can now become author, publisher, printer and distributor of your own products!

There are many software programs that allow you to design your own CD-ROM labels and J-cards for placing in the CD-ROM jewel cases.

Even with an inexpensive color ink jet or laser printer, you can create professional and attractive CD-ROM eBook packages.

The URL for Amazon.com's Advantage Program is at:

http://www.amazon.com/advantage

Once your CD-ROM has a valid ISBN number and you have registered it properly in the Bowker Books-In-Print directory, you will receive a free listing in the Borders.com, and Barnes & Noble on-line book catalogs.

You will then need to add cover art and commentary to your free listing.

I believe that soon, Borders.com will be including Adobe Acrobat PDF eBooks so it will be wise to add eBook listings to their catalog.

Borders.com is located at:

http://www.borders.com

Summary:

Make sure you have back up systems to support your eBook business. The Internet is flaky. You will experience delays and problems with transmissions. However, the more back up systems you have in place, the easier it will become to service your customers.

Think about adding a CD-ROM Re-writer to your computer hardware. The cost less than $300.00 and can be used like a printing press to manufacture your eBooks in CD-ROM versions. You can even custom design your packaging to create a very attractive product

Chapter Seven

eBook Publishing and Marketing Resources

These are resources that will be updated periodically for your benefit.

Use these resources to achieve success in selling your eBooks. When you send in the eBook registration information located in the appendix, you will receive instructions on how to receive regular updated chapters in this book.

Where do I go to obtain United States Copyright forms?

Click on the link below to find your copyright forms and information.

http://www.loc.gov/copyright/

Where do I get my ISBN numbers?

Once you get your copyright you need to obtain an ISBN number. In order for your eBook to be listed on Amazon.com, Barnes & Noble.com, Borders.com and other Internet bookstores, you must have ISBN numbers.

The ISBN number is needed if you produce a printed and bound version of your book or a on CD-ROM.

The book will then be listed in a publication titled *Books-In-Print*.

Libraries and bookstores refer to *Books-In-Print* when they need to special order a book from a publisher.

Books-In-Print includes listings for RocketEditions, Softbook Editions, CD-ROM's and PDF digital files.

I feel *Books-In-Print* will be getting a great amount of use in the coming years. Now is a great time to be including your eBooks in this reference publication.

How many ISBN numbers do I need?

For each binding, such as Adobe Acrobat format, Microsoft Word Format, Rocketbook, Softbook, Glassbook, etc, you need a separate ISBN number.

Every time you change a book cover, binding or update your book, you need a new ISBN number.

Even if you are only planning to publish one book, I recommend you obtain several ISBN numbers. As of the writing the fee for a block of 100 numbers is the same as the fee for just one.

Click on the link below to apply for your numbers.

http://www.bowker.com

What software do I need to publish eBooks?

You can author eBooks with the following software.

Microsoft Word

Word Perfect

Microsoft Reader

Adobe Acrobat

You can find all of these products on-line at my bookstore located at:

http://www.eBook-marketing.com

You can use a free copy of Adobe Acrobat when you publish on-line to format your first eBooks at the following Internet location:

http://createpdf.adobe.com/

You also have the choice of buying the Adobe Acrobat Software or you can lease it for $9.95 per month.

When you have your first eBooks published you may want to purchase the Adobe Acrobat Software.

Purchase the latest version because Adobe is very committed to the eBook publishing business.

Adobe Acrobat is one of the standard eBook authoring software packages.

There are many ways to publish eBooks. Keep in mind that with the many different computer operating systems and many different pieces of hardware to interact with, you need a software product that can communicate well with others. Adobe Acrobat communicates well.

On top of that, if you ever want to turn your book into a printed and bound copy, Adobe is on of the standards in the pre-press book printing industry. The investment you make in this software will be a wise one for you.

Just recently Adobe has begun offering a monthly rental of its software. This is a great idea because you have a low monthly investment and you will be getting all of the latest up-grades.

Chapter Three: How to Publish Your eBook in One Day

Once you are published on the Internet check out Angela Adair-Hoy's Booklocker. This is a great place to sell your eBooks. Angela is dedicated to the eBook publishing business. She has been offered to have her books printed and bound in exchange for giving up her electronic rights.

She said "No way." Angela is earning more money and keeping more money by self-publishing her own eBooks.

If you want to pay someone to create your eBooks and sell them on-line, then go to 1stbooks Library. I have my books selling on the 1stbooks Library Website and I am very pleased with their services.

Check out other eBook publishing and eBook selling sites to expand your market. You will find a ton of information at eBooknet.com including forums you may want to join.

Writerswrite.com and iuniverse.com are also great resources on eBook publishing and marketing.

Chapter Four:

Marketing Your First eBook with No Budget

Using Fingertip Marketing to Sell Your Books

What books do you recommend I purchase that will help me market with no marketing budget?

Every book that John Kremer creates about book publishing is something I personally buy and use. I have been to his workshops and I have learned a great deal from him. He is dedicated in helping you achieve your book publishing goals.

He has a book titled *1001 Ways to Market Your Books*.

Many of the "1001 Ways" can be used to market your eBooks.

1001 Ways to Market Your Book by John Kremer

ISBN 0-912411-48-1

John's book is the best book you can purchase on book and eBook marketing. His website is more than just a catalog listing. He has more free marketing resources than anyone involved in any kind of marketing.

You will find additional eBook marketing information on Angela Adair-Hoy's Booklocker.com website.

Angela is a pioneer in the eBook publishing and eBook selling market place. She has a wonderful book titled, *How to Write, Sell and Publish eBooks*

While you are at it, go back to her website when you are ready to e-publish your masterpiece. You can earn 70% royalties by listing your eBook with her. Steven King will be jealous.

Where can I find a list of e-zines that may want to read a sample chapter of my eBook?

Learn how to create your own e-zines from the E-zine University at:

http://www.ezineuniversity.com/

Find tons of e-zine information here.

http://www.zinebook.com

Here is a place you can post your articles in exchange for links back to your website or other eBook ordering websites. You can also find free content here for your own e-zine.

http://www.ezinearticles.com/

The following directory is a great source.

http://www.meer.net/~johnl/e-zine-list/index.html

The following is a web-ring for e-zines.

http://ezinewebring.hypermart.net/

Chapter Five: What You Need To Sell eBooks From Your Website

Where do I go to have my website hosted?

My first choice is Valueweb.

Valueweb is located at:

http://www.valueweb.net

I don't have a second choice!

Ask people you know and trust "who hosts your website and are you satisfied with their customer service?"

Remember to stay away from free web sites. You can create more marketing muscle through your own personal website than all of the free one's put together.

The only time you should be using free websites are to host articles you have written for others.

Spend your time wisely on promoting your own website. If you have lots of time on your hands use the same promotional techniques to promote the URLs at Internet eBooksellers that are listing your eBook.

Domain name registration.

You will need to register your domain. If you don't choose any of the above hosting companies, here is a direct link to registering your domain.

http://www.networksolutions.com/

Resource: Autoresponders

Websites that offer free autoresponders. First use your website hosting company. If you don't have one yet you can still obtain these amazing marketing tools. The autoresponder is the ***greatest Internet marketing tool*** you will ever find.

http://www.fastfacts.net/

http://www.smartbotpro.net/newsite2/features.html

http://www.infoback.net/

http://www.sendfree.com

Meta Tags For Your Website

How to create META tags. Use the following links to help you get this very important job done correctly.

http://www.searchenginewatch.com/

Chapter Six: Setting Up Back-up Systems.

Credit Card Processing

Always use a back up system for credit card processing. I use CCSLIDE as my main back up system because there is no monthly minimum transactions and no monthly fees. Check them out.

http://www.ccslide.com

Clickbank.com is a great one I just heard about.

Clickbank.com offers an extensive affiliate program. They have over 30000 merchants that may just refer their customers over to your website!

Check out the option for digital content with no merchant account status necessary. It is a good deal.

http://www.clickbank.com

Pay2SEE

Here is a neat concept. You can have these guys do your credit card fulfillment and even set up and store your download page with up to 10 eBooks for only $99.00!

You can use the Pay2SEE system of credit card acceptance and eBook fulfillment. You do not need to set up a secure Merchant Account. Pay2SEE will process the transactions and pay royalties on your work.

Back up your data often using compact disc technology or tape back up systems. You want to back up and save everything you place on your website host's server. In 5 years of using Value Web I have never lost any data but I don't want any unpleasant surprises.

The BookZone

Mary Westheimer's BookZone offers a total solution for eBooks. The BookZone can create secured ordering, encrypted eBooks and can design your website as well.

They have designed many publisher and author websites.

List of Electronic Publishers and eBooksellers To Contact.

Some Internet eBook publishers and eBook sellers charge fees and some do not. Read all contracts carefully!

Watch for the word "exclusive" and "non-exclusive."

I personally would never assign my electronic rights on an "exclusive" basis because then I would be tied to the marketing efforts of only that one electronic eBook seller.

No one has a lock on the eBook selling market.

Think of each eBook publisher and eBook seller as individual brick and mortar bookstores.

As soon as you are 50 miles away, you begin to find new bookstores to purchase your books.

Would you offer your books at only one or two neighborhood stores?

There are hundreds, maybe even thousands of websites selling books. Why not be listed on as many of them as possible?

Summary:

Well, there you have it. You are ready to embark on a wonderful journey that may earn you some great money.

Remember that most Internet businesses are making very little money if any.

You as an eBook author/publisher have the best opportunity of any business selling over the Internet to make a profit.

Digital files are cheap. Once you make them, they are easy to create and duplicate. You do not have inventory problems like traditional businesses.

The best part about marketing your eBooks is the fact that there are many people located in countries you may have never heard of that are waiting for you to share your story with them.

You live in the most exciting time in human history! You can communicate with people the world over, and share your experiences and your life with them.

Begin today and participate in this exciting time!

We have more to accomplish in this book including how to get your eBooks published as traditional books.

Let's move on

Chapter Eight

Publishing eBooks on eBook Reading Devices

Did you realize that thousands of people are reading their eBooks on dedicated eBook reading devices? These devices simulate the traditional book reading environment and allow the reader an enhanced experience.

The reader can download several eBooks to a book reader, make notes in margins and read from a back lit screen while in bed at night.

In addition, eBook readers allow you to change the print fonts and character size, allowing you to facilitate the reading experience.

I am only going to mention the top three eBook reading devices but will include more in updates when I find it necessary.

The three dedicated eBook-reading devices are the Rocketbook, Everybook and the Softbook.

Note: Update: September 26, 2000 The Rocketbook and Softbook are combining forces and will look different then the specifications given in this chapter. I am still including this chapter to give you a little historical perspective on eBooks and eBook readers.

eBook 2, *How to Write A Best-selling eBook* will include more current information.

Rocketbook:

Rocketbook by NuvoMedia is fantastic!

A Rocket Book is an eBook-reading device that can hold 40 or more complete books. It is available now and you can order a Rocketbook from Barnes & Noble and Powells.com Internet bookstores.

The Rocketbook is the true leader in the industry.

Rocketbook by NuvoMedia is very user friendly for the eBook publisher.

For example, as soon as I complete writing an eBook and send the files to the NuvoMedia's Rocket Press, my book will be ready for international distribution within 24-48 hours!

I can update my books as often as I wish enabling the Rocketbook customer a rich and new reading experience.

Currently an author must have an established relationship as a "publisher" with NuvoMedia to take advantage of selling eBooks as Rocket Editions. There are many eBook publishers, however, that will take your eBook, format it for the Rocketbook eBook Reader, and then send you the royalties when your Rocket Editions are downloaded from eBook sellers.

1stbooks.com is a great company that will format your eBook for a Rocket Edition and make it available to sell on Barnes & Noble and Powells.com.

1stbooks is located at:

http://www.1stbooks.com

I personally sell more Rocket Editions of my eBooks than with any other eBook seller or publisher.

If you are a single title author, you will need to contact a publisher that will format the Rocket Editions for you. I have indicated publishers that will do that for you in Chapter Seven and in Chapter Ten.

If you have published 10 titles or more and issue your own ISBN numbers, you can contact the Director of Content of NuvoMedia at:

http://www.nuvomedia.com

NuvoMedia's address is:

310 Villa Street
Mt. View, CA 94041
(650) 314-1200
(650) 314-1201 (fax)

Everybook:

Everybook represents the future of eBook reading devices. It has everything!

The Everybook can hold 260 Megabytes of storage on a single card. Since most books you find at the bookstore translate into less than one Megabyte, you can see that each Everybook eBook Reader can hold hundreds of books.

Each Everybook eBook Reader includes two full color screens that simulate an 8 1/2 by 11-inch book.

Turning of pages is also simulated to remind the user of a traditional book reading experience.

Both screens are in full color!

My personal feeling is that the Everybook will be a wonderful asset for college students.

Imagine registering for college courses. Your advisor gives you a class schedule for your freshman year.

You go to the college bookstore where you pay for your Everybook and then download all of your textbooks. You will also download monographs and required readings for those courses at kiosks located in the bookstore.

During the school year you will be able to read your assignments and print out questions and answers at the end of each chapter. You will have room to store additional books and documents as well.

College textbooks will be priced much cheaper because of the savings over traditional print runs, storage and distribution costs.

Professors will be encouraged to write updated books and will be able to have a shorter turnaround time in book production.

Full motion audio and video will be included which will make this eBook-reading device a fantastic reading experience.

Everybook may become a top player in the eBook market.

Contact them and see if they want to include your eBook in their catalog.

Everybook is located out of Middletown, PA which is near the state capital of Pennsylvania.

Everybook's Internet address is:

http://www.everybook.net

Softbook:

The Softbook eBook Reader is one of the pioneers in the industry.

All you need is a telephone line to hook up as each device includes a modem to download books directly into the reader.

Currently thousands of eBook as well as magazines are included for the Softbook eBook Reader.

Each device includes sophisticated searching, bookmarking, hyperlinking, text markup and a stylus for marking and highlighting.

Contact the director of content and find out how you can include your new eBook in their bookstore.

Softbook Press is located at:

http://www.softbook.com

Headquarters

Softbook Press
900 Island Drive
Redwood City, California 94065-5150
(650) 620-4100 telephone
(650) 632-1807 fax

Summary:

Now you can expand your eBook offerings by contacting companies that market dedicated eBook-reading devices.

The Rocketbook, Everybook, and Softbook are the major players in the dedicated eBook reading device industry today.

We can only imagine how the industry will change and advance over time.

Make sure you check out all of the possibilities of publishing your eBooks with the eBook reader companies.

Chapter Nine

How to Turn Your eBooks into Bound Books

When you begin telling all of your friends and family about the fact that you are now a "published" author you are going to hear a response like, "when are you going to publish a real book?"

Some individuals will never get over the fact that publishing is changing very quickly. Electronic books are taking over.

Now you can publish your bound books on-demand and never have to worry about getting stuck with a garage full of excess inventory.

This is the next best thing to publishing an eBook!

Books-on-demand are the digital files taken from your eBooks that are converted and turned into trade paperback books. In the publishing industry when books are published on demand the publisher of that style of book is called a POD. He is a Print-On-Demand publisher.

Print-On-Demand books look exactly like any 5"x7," 6"x9" or 8 1/2" x11" books, that you find selling in any traditional brick and mortar bookstore.

The major difference is that the POD books were printed one at a time. Instead of using an offset printing press, the book pages were digitized and stored in a high quality copy machine, collated and then perfect bound on another machine.

One of the largest book wholesalers, Ingram, provides books on demand to bookstores and distributors throughout the world.

What this means is that if you can somehow get your eBook printed on demand and placed into the Ingram data base, people can order your book from almost any bookstore and have it delivered within a day or two.

The book does not sit in a warehouse collecting dust and becoming a warehousing problem. The book is printed as it is ordered.

Since publishing on-demand realizes huge savings for bookstores and distributors everywhere, books on demand printed by the POD's are becoming very popular.

Internet bookstores like Amazon.com and Barnes & Noble cut into the sales of traditional bookstores.

The major reason is that they can carry many more titles. A typical brick and mortar bookstore cannot afford to invest and inventory every book in print.

Internet bookstores can order from one centralized location and make special ordering of books very efficient for their customers.

As book wholesalers like Ingram carry more POD titles, they will be able to service bookstores in a much more efficient manner. Book wholesalers will be able to carry a greater variety of books as well as providing publishing and delivery of books within a day or two.

Soon Print-On-Demand books will be available at the bookstore level as well.

Make sure you follow this industry very closely!

So, how can you participate in getting your eBook sold in a printed-on-demand environment? Where can you get it produced for a reasonable cost and at the same time get national distribution?

How can you keep your print and electronic publishing rights to capitalize on opportunities that will present themselves very soon?

Your questions will be answered in Chapter Ten.

Summary:

Print-On-Demand books allow you to expand into a huge market without the huge financial risk associated with traditional book printing.

Print-On-Demand books are available at the wholesale level with Ingram, one of the largest book wholesalers in the world.

Print-On-Demand machines will soon be available in many bookstores as well.

Make sure you check out this option for publishing your books!

Chapter Ten

A One Source Solution for eBooks, eBook Readers Paperbound Books and More!

I know what you are thinking. "Boy this is a great deal of work for me to do, just to sell books." "Maybe I can just get on Oprah's television show and I will be set for life."

The truth is that even if you get on Oprah's television show, you are still going to have to work hard at selling and promoting your eBooks. *A Cheap and Easy Guide to Self-publishing E-books,* will help you get started. The daily marketing plan I present will have you completing just three activities a day for five days each week.

You can still maintain a full-time job while you are completing these marketing activities.

All of the book marketing activities involve letting "your fingers do the talking" rather than requiring you to call or meet someone in person. Once you have your first eBook published on-line, you are ready to tackle a single source solution for eBook publishing that will increase your current eBook sales, give you additional eBook media to market, and turn your eBook into a printed and bound book.

The best total solution that I have found is the *1stbooks Library.*

They are located at:

http://www.1stbooks.com

Address:

1stbooks Library

2511 West Third Street, Suite 1

Bloomington, IN 47404

Phone: (800)-839-8640

Fax: (812)-339-6554

E-mail: 1stbooks@1stbooks.com

The 1stbooks Library can help you in the following ten ways:

1. Publish your eBooks

For a reasonable fee they will turn your finished document into an eBook. They will assign their own ISBN number to it and have it listed in Books-In-Print. You can still offer your eBooks to be sold by the Booklocker, Mightywords.com or any other on-line eBook seller that sell non-exclusively. 1stbooks Library will allow you to retain your electronic and print rights. The 1stbooks Library publishing contract is non-exclusive.

2. List Your eBooks In the 1stbooks Library Bookstore

Yes, it is always nice to have another bookstore listing for your eBooks. I first discovered the 1stbooks Library by conducting a search for "eBooks" on the Yahoo search directory. Since 1stbooks came up first on the Yahoo listing, I knew the 1stbooks Library was expert in Internet marketing. They had the "post position" being the first eBook publisher listed. I felt that their bookstore would receive more page views than any other eBook seller would.

People get tired of scrolling down their computer screen and looking through many choices during an Internet search.

Always make note of which website is coming up first in your search results. You may want to join up with them later.

Now, over a year later, 1stbooks Library still has that "post position" on the Yahoo search directory. There are over 4000 eBooks listed on the 1stbooks Library and more to come. They want to be known as the Amazon.com of Internet eBook Stores

3. Format and Sell Your Rocketbook Editions

Again, for a reasonable fee, 1stbooks Library will format and market your Rocketeditions. This will allow you to sell Rocketeditions even if you don't have a publishing relationship with NuvoMedia.

Rocketeditions of books are selling like crazy. I personally sell more Rocketeditions on Barnes & Noble and Powells.com than just about any other eBook media. Don't overlook this wonderful eBook selling opportunity!

I am predicting by the end of the year 2000, hundreds of thousands of people will own Rocketbooks. Many of these people will be looking for your eBook as a Rocketedition.

4. Print and Bind Your eBooks

1stbooks Library has a unique system of taking your eBooks, printing and binding them on demand. You are allowed to purchase as few or as many books as you need at a wholesale price.

Now you will have a printed and bound book that looks like all of the other perfect bound trade paperback books stocked in bookstores and libraries.

You will receive a unique ISBN number as well. Your new books will be listed in Books-In-Print, which is a major reference for bookstores and libraries.

Your book will be available at the 1stbooks Library. Your book will now have two listings, doubling its exposure at the 1stbooks Library on-line bookstore. You will be listed as an eBook for download and as a trade paperback to be shipped via mail or United Parcel Service to your customer.

Generally an order placed to 1stbooks Library's website will just take a few days to process and your printed and bound version will be sent out to the customer.

By the way, the packaging of your book will be quality packaging, just like Amazon.com. Your customer will receive the book in tiptop shape.

1stbooks Library will handle the credit card transactions and give you reports on what you have sold through their system.

They will also pay you royalties that are much greater than standard book publishing royalties.

Now you will have a "real book" to impress your friends and neighbors. Hey and maybe even Oprah!

5. Place Your Printed and Bound Version in the Ingram Database.

One solid fact about getting a bookstore to carry your books is that you need to have a working relationship with a large book distributor or book wholesaler.

Librarians and bookstores want and need the services of large distributors and wholesalers.

They do not want to write thousands of checks to authors and small publishers each month, but they do want to carry their titles.

Wholesalers and distributors enable bookstores to carry thousands of books and only a few checks have to be written. They also help control the inventory costs of each store.

Ingram is one of best known and reliable wholesalers in the bookstore and library acquisition world. Along with a standard Books-In Print reference book that most bookstores and libraries use, Ingram provides their own version of Books-In-Print.

Once you are in Ingram's database, you can approach bookstores for signings and libraries to purchase your books.

Also, when Ingram gets an order from a library or bookstore, they will have your book printed on demand and shipped to the store within three to five days. Lightning Print is the name of Ingram's service that provides such a fast turnaround on small book orders.

This is much quicker than the two weeks or four weeks quote you will receive when a bookstore has to deal directly with a standard book publisher.

1stbooks provides the electronic files including the book covers to Ingram's Lightning Print system and the books are printed on-demand. The probability of handling costly returns is very minimal.

This print-on-demand technology will help bookstores and libraries carry more books and reduce storage and inventory costs.

6. Get Your Book Printed on Demand at Store Locations throughout the United States!

This is really exciting. Sprout, a digital printing company out of Atlanta, Georgia, is involved in providing digital printing systems to bookstores.

Current stores that will be using Sprout's Print-On-Demand system are selected Borders, Waldenbooks, Follett, and other selected bookstores in the United States.

Once you are in the 1stbooks family, you will be able to have your book distributed as an electronic file to a bookstore serviced with the Sprout digital publishing system. On location and right at the bookstore, your book will be printed out while the customer waits.

The turn around time is only 15 minutes!

7. Availability on Amazon.com and Other Internet Bookstores

Everyone that publishes a book wants to be listed on Amazon.com. Amazon.com is the King of Internet bookstores. They have a great reputation for customer service and delivery of products. They are around to stay. By having your printed and bound version published by the 1stbooks Library your book will be sold on Amazon.com, Barnes & Noble, borders.com, fatbrain.com and other Canadian Internet bookstores like Indiago.ca and Chapters.ca.

My book, *How To Hypnotize Yourself Without Losing Your Mind* is being sold on Amazon.co.uk which is located in the United Kingdom and Amazon.de, which is located in Germany.

This is all because of the fact that Ingram entered my 1stbooks trade paper back in the foreign marketplace.

If your eBooks and print on demand books are listed on the Internet bookstore websites readers will perceive you as a genuine author.

8. Special Market Sales Print Runs.

One way an author can sell thousands of copies of paperback books without having to worry about returns is by selling in special markets.

Special markets include selling to book clubs and selling books to multi-level marketing organizations. Special markets also include selling books as premiums to associations and corporations.

Many times when a special market or premium sale is made, the quantity of books ordered can amount in the tens of thousands.

A typical print-on-demand publisher will not be able to offer competitive enough prices to accommodate such an order since POD works with copy machines rather than true printing presses.

1stbook Library, however, will work through their resources and help you put a competitive deal together for your special market and premium sales clients.

Many self-published authors earn their living from special market book sales. Having access to a full service publisher is a very important benefit for you to consider when choosing a print-on-demand resource.

9. Audiobooks or books- on-tape production and distribution.

Yes, 1stbooks has a program that will take your book and turn it into a book on tape or an audiobook.

People love to listen to books on tape while commuting to and from work. Many listen to books while exercising. As people are living longer and with their eyesight failing with age, audiobooks allow them to continue enjoying books.

1stbook library has an option for authors and publishers to create books-on-tape. They will set up distribution through the Ingram database that will facilitate sales to bookstores and libraries.

10. Publicity and promotional help.

There is another publishing package option offered by the 1stbooks Library that can get the author off to a great start.

This option focuses on sending targeted press releases about your new books. When your new softcover book or book on tape is ready, 1stbooks Library will send hundreds of press releases to media in your region.

From news releases you may receive requests for review copies of your books and possibly radio and TV interviews. 1stbooks library will help you work with these new adventures.

Media interviews can really help all of your book sales increase dramatically.

Summary:

Once you have your first eBooks published and you are marketing on-line, consider having your book sold as a book-on-demand.

If you don't want to do all the work of publishing your eBooks on-line, contract with 1stbooks Library to handle all of the work in publishing and distribution of your works.

The 1stbooks Library has a turnkey operation that will help you create and sell eBooks in a variety of ways. They will print your book in softcover and instantly acquire wholesale distribution channels for your books.

You will become a "real" author and at the same time, not have to worry about inventory costs and other high costs associated with the traditional book-publishing world.

We wish you success!

www.ingramcontent.com/pod-product-compliance
Lightning Source LLC
Chambersburg PA
CBHW081421080526
44589CB00016B/2621